# Briefly: Kant's *Groundwork of the Metaphysics of Morals*

GW00468904

# Briefly: Kant's *Groundwork of the Metaphysics of Morals*

David Mills Daniel

scm press

© David Mills Daniel 2006

The author and publisher acknowledge material reproduced
from M. Gregor, trans. and ed., *Kant: Groundwork of the
Metaphysics of Morals*, 1998, Cambridge University Press.
Reprinted by permission of Cambridge University Press.
All rights reserved.

British Library Cataloguing in Publication data

A catalogue record for this book is available
from the British Library

0 334 04026 4/9780 334 04026 2

First published in 2006 by SCM Press
9–17 St Alban's Place,
London N1 0NX

www.scm-canterburypress.co.uk

SCM Press is a division of
SCM-Canterbury Press Ltd

Printed and bound in Great Britain by
CPD (Wales) Ltd, Ebbw Vale

**To My Parents**

# Contents

# Introduction

The SCM *Briefly* series is designed to enable students and general readers to acquire knowledge and understanding of key texts in philosophy, philosophy of religion, theology and ethics. While the series will be especially helpful to those following university and A-level courses in philosophy, ethics and religious studies, it will in fact be of interest to anyone looking for a short guide to the ideas of a particular philosopher or theologian.

Each book in the series takes a piece of work by one philosopher and provides a summary of the original text, which adheres closely to it, and includes direct quotations from it, thus enabling the reader to follow each development in the philosopher's argument(s). Throughout the summary, there are page references to the original philosophical writing, so that the reader has ready access to the primary text. In the Introduction to each book, you will find details of the edition of the philosophical work referred to.

In *Briefly: Kant's Groundwork of the Metaphysics of Morals*, we refer to Immanuel Kant, *Groundwork of the Metaphysics of Morals*, edited by M. Gregor, Cambridge: Cambridge University Press, 1998, ISBN 0521626951.

Each *Briefly* begins with an Introduction, followed by a chapter on the Context in which the work was written. Who was this writer? Why was this book written? With some Issues to Consider, and some Suggested Further Reading, this *Briefly* aims to get anyone started in their philosophical investigation. The detailed summary of the philosophical work is followed by a concise chapter-by-chapter overview and an extensive glossary of terms.

All words that appear in the Glossary are highlighted in bold type the first time that they appear in the Detailed Summary and the Overview of this *Briefly* guide. However, it should be noted that some words in the Detailed Summary appear in bold in the edition on which it is based.

# Context

## Who was Immanuel Kant?

Immanuel Kant, whose ideas on metaphysics, moral philosophy and the philosophy of religion have had such a profound and lasting influence on thinking in all these areas, was born in Königsberg, East Prussia, in 1724. Although Kant did not come from a wealthy background (his father was a saddler), he was able to become a student at the University of Königsberg in 1740, where he showed an interest in science and astronomy as well as philosophy. After graduating, Kant worked as a tutor for a number of years, before returning to Königsberg as a private lecturer at the university in 1755. He was appointed professor of logic and metaphysics in 1770. In many ways, Kant's life is exactly what we would expect that of a professional philosopher to be. In addition to his teaching responsibilities at the university, where his lectures covered such subjects as physics, geography and anthropology, he devoted himself almost entirely to study, thought and writing. In order to use his time efficiently, he rose before five o'clock in the morning, and followed an unvarying daily routine, allocating fixed periods of time to each activity. His first major work of philosophy, the *Critique of Pure Reason*, was published in 1781. His other books include: *Prolegomena to any Future Metaphysic* (1783), *Groundwork of the Metaphysics of Morals* (1785), the second edition of the *Critique of Pure Reason* (1787), *Critique of Practical Reason* (1788) and *Religion within the Boundaries of Mere Reason* (1793). Kant died in 1804.

## What is the *Groundwork of the Metaphysics of Morals*?

In the preface to the *Groundwork*, Kant tells us that the book's purpose is to discover the supreme principle of morality, which, he believes, will not be found in human nature, or in any part of our ordinary experience, but *a priori*, in our reason. What Kant provides in the *Groundwork* is a deontological system of morals: that is, a moral system in which actions are right or wrong in themselves, and where moral principles (what Kant calls the moral law) are followed for their own sake, and not because of their consequences, or because they are believed to meet specific human needs.

Kant begins by maintaining that only a good will is good without limitation. What Kant means by a good will is one that seeks to carry out moral duties for their own sake, and not for personal advantage, to satisfy desires or inclinations, or because of their consequences. Kant illustrates his point with examples. First, he considers a shopkeeper, who refrains from overcharging his customers. But does his conduct have moral worth? His honest behaviour may be due to a desire to retain his customers, rather than the duty not to cheat them. The other example is of a philanthropist, who is out of sympathy with humanity, but who continues his charitable acts, despite the fact that they are contrary to his inclinations. There can be no doubt that his actions have moral worth.

Kant is making a number of points here. He is saying that, in order to do the right thing, we sometimes have to act against our inclinations. He is saying that it is sometimes hard to tell whether people are doing the right thing for the right reasons, as opposed to self-interested ones. He also seems to be saying that actions that are contrary to our inclinations have more moral worth than those that are not, even if the right thing is done. In the example of the philanthropist, he considers those who delight in helping others. For such people, helping others fits in with their inclinations, so their actions lack true moral worth.

But the really important point Kant is making is that an action's moral worth lies in the maxim, or rule of conduct, upon which it is decided, not in its consequences. An action that excludes any personal inclination or consideration of consequences will be right because it will be determined only by the *a priori* moral law that comes from the reason. For the will to be absolutely good, it must be determined by what Kant calls universal law as such: 'I ought never to act except in such a way that I could also will that my maxim should become a universal law.'

Again, Kant provides an example: that of a man in difficulties, who contemplates making a false promise, in order to get himself out of them. Kant argues that a maxim of not making a false promise, because it would mean not being trusted in future, would be based on consequences, which is not the same as being truthful from duty. However, the maxim of making false promises when in difficulties could not become a universal law, because it would destroy itself: a universal law to lie would end all promises, as it would be pointless to make them. But, although there does seem to be a contradiction between the concept of a promise (undertaking to do something) and a universal law allowing false promises (undertaking to do what you have no intention of doing), Kant's example also seems to point to consequences: the undermining of confidence in promises, if such a maxim becomes universal.

3

## Context

While some of what Kant has to say here is relatively easy to accept, other parts of it are not. We recognize that doing the right thing will often involve going against our own inclinations, and that this is a factor that enters into our judgement of the moral worth of an action. We are more likely to applaud actions that involve some sacrifice of the agent's inclinations than those where the agent does what he wants to do anyway, even if we regard the course of action chosen as morally right. But are we prepared to exclude all consideration of consequences from our moral decision-making? Quite apart from the influence on our moral thinking of utilitarianism (and the connection between moral decisions and promoting happiness), human needs, and the consequences of our actions in relation to satisfying those needs, do seem to play a big part in our decisions about what is right and wrong and which courses of action we should follow.

Kant has reasons for rejecting consequences and human nature as the basis of morality, which he develops later in the *Groundwork*, but he has made a point which it is difficult, even for those who disagree with much of his moral philosophy, to reject: that moral principles apply universally. People should not perform an action unless they can will that the maxims by which they act should become a universal law: the moral principles they adopt should apply for all people (rational beings, as Kant calls them) in all situations. Therefore, if supposed moral principles are put forward, which apply only to some people or particular circumstances, or which favour some groups or individuals rather than others, that is a reason to challenge them.

Kant has made it clear that moral principles cannot be grounded in human nature. Why is this? It is because the conditions of humanity are contingent. The way that human beings are depends on a range of empirical factors, which could have been different, and which may change in the future; Kant, however, is looking for moral principles that will be valid for all rational beings, irrespective of any purely empirical factors. Therefore, they must be derived from the reason, not from human experience.

One response would be that, as human beings are the only rational beings that concern us, or which exist (as far as we know), we should relate our moral principles to (satisfying) human needs. However, Kant has an important point, even for those who do base their moral principles on human needs. While there are common human needs, differences among human beings mean that (at least some of) their needs differ. This applies even to the purpose that Kant acknowledges all human beings pursue: happiness. It is an indeterminate concept, because different people include different things in their idea of happiness, and it depends upon empirical elements, which cannot be guaranteed in either the present or the future. Therefore, any attempt to link morality to promotion of happiness is bound to fail. Again, if we try to base morality on what human beings, or particular groups of human beings, actually consider to be right or wrong, we have to recognize that their views may be influenced by their own inclinations, desires or self-interest.

Kant explores the way that morality works. Only rational beings possess a will and the ability to act according to moral principles that come from the reason. However, in human beings, inclination and interest may be at variance with the moral law, so it is expressed in commands or imperatives. For imperfect human beings, whose wills are influenced by their inclinations, morality is presented as things that they ought to do. However, a divine or holy will would not need imperatives, because, free of inclinations, it would already be in accord with the moral law.

Kant explains the difference between hypothetical and moral imperatives. The former are conditional, indicating actions that are necessary in order to achieve an end that is optional. But moral imperatives are unconditional or categorical: they command actions that are necessary in themselves. And there is only one categorical imperative: 'act only in accordance with that maxim through which you can at the same time will that it become a universal law', which can also be expressed as: 'act as if the maxim of your action were to become by your will a universal law of nature'. In *Utilitarianism*, Mill argues that this principle could result in adoption of 'outrageously immoral rules of conduct'. In fact, this first formulation of the categorical imperative enables us to test our maxims. If they cannot function as universal moral laws, applicable to all rational beings, they should be rejected.

However, while this sounds fine in theory, the examples Kant gives do not work particularly well. He considers a man who is prospering, but who sees that others are not. However, he follows his inclination, which is to look after himself, and to ignore the problems of others. Kant accepts that humanity would be able to survive adoption of this maxim, but it could not be willed as a universal law, because it would be in conflict with itself, ruling out the possibility of the help which everyone needs at times. However, it is hard not to feel that the root objection to this maxim is that it would have such undesirable consequences.

But why should we bother to be moral at all? Kant observes that the will is determined by an end. However, most of the ends that we pursue have only relative worth, in relation to achieving particular desires. Therefore, they cannot be the

source of universal moral principles and categorical imperatives. What is needed is something that is an end in itself, and
which has absolute worth. And the only things which have
absolute worth are human and all rational beings, yielding
another formulation of the categorical imperative: 'So act that
you use humanity, whether in your own or in the person of
another, always at the same time as an end, never merely as a
means.'

Again, regardless of the view that is taken of Kant's moral
philosophy as a whole, it is hard to see what else could be the
basis of morality. Even if we believe that actions are right or
wrong to the extent that they promote happiness, why should
we be concerned about other people's happiness, as opposed to
concentrating exclusively on our own, unless we attach some
value to other human beings? Kant, of course, goes much further. Human beings have absolute worth, and every maxim
we adopt should lead only to actions that always treat human
beings as ends in themselves, and never simply as means to
achieving our own ends. Again, Kant gives examples, including that of the man who makes a false promise. Such a man
uses the person to whom he makes the promise as a means,
not an end. Kant provides a compelling image of how we
should discharge our moral responsibilities with his idea of all
rational beings regarding themselves as members of a kingdom of ends, acting as if they are adopting maxims which are
to serve as universal laws for all rational beings, and treating
themselves, and others, as ends not means.

For Kant, the autonomy of the will is the supreme principle
of morals, while heteronomy of the will is the source of all
spurious moral principles. Heteronomy of the will arises
when, in making moral decisions, people allow their will to be
determined by considerations other than the fitness of their

maxims to serve as universal laws for all rational beings. The obvious sources of spurious moral principles are empirical factors, such as human desires and inclinations. The example Kant gives is of someone who adopts the maxim of not lying, not because lying is wrong, but because of a desire to preserve his reputation. However, heteronomy would also arise if moral principles were taken from an all-perfect divine will. Kant's point is that morality is autonomous: things are not right just because they satisfy certain desires, maximize happiness, or even because they reflect the will of God. If they were, then moral decision-making would involve only deciding whether or not a particular course of action will promote happiness, or please God; and there could be no question as to whether what promotes happiness or pleases God is right.

To be autonomous is to be free, and Kant maintains that, in order to have wills which are their own, and to be able to adopt as maxims universal principles, to which they hold themselves subject, rational beings (and, therefore, human beings) must be free. But what proof is there that we are actually free, when we know that we are subject to the causality of laws of nature? Kant's answer is that we cannot prove that we are free, any more than we can prove the existence of categorical imperatives. However, he distinguishes between the world of sense (that is, things as they appear to us, because of the kind of beings we are), of which our senses give us knowledge, and within which our actions are determined by desires and inclinations, and the world of understanding (that is, things as they are in themselves), to which, because we possess reason, human (and all rational) beings belong. Therefore, we have two standpoints from which to view our relationship with the moral law. As part of the world of sense, we are subject to laws of nature, but as part of the world of understanding, we are subject to moral laws, which come from the reason and are independent of nature. However, because, as part of the world of sense, our actions are determined by desires and inclinations, moral laws have to be expressed as imperatives.

Kant acknowledges the difficulties of this analysis, because the freedom claimed seems to contradict the natural necessity of laws of nature, and, while freedom is only an idea of reason, laws of nature are an objective reality. Indeed, Kant admits that there is no possibility of explaining matters that are not determined by laws of nature, so the limit of moral enquiry has been reached. However, as we cannot give up the idea of freedom (which is essential, if there is going to be moral responsibility), we have to accept that, although we cannot explain it, there actually is no contradiction between holding that beings, who are subject to the laws of nature, are also independent of them, and subject to moral laws given by pure reason.

Kant's moral system, as set out in the *Groundwork*, is not straightforward, and getting to grips with it is not helped by Kant's complex, and sometimes opaque, style of writing. However, it does repay the effort made. Kant has a lot to offer, and even those who do not accept his moral system in its entirety cannot deny his important contribution to moral philosophy. We may feel that consideration of human needs, and of the consequences of our actions, cannot be (wholly) excluded from moral decision-making, but Kant makes us aware of the dangers of basing our moral principles on human desires, including happiness, or on what human beings consider to be right or wrong at a particular point in history. Again, unless human beings are free, they cannot be held morally responsible for their actions. Finally, it is difficult to see why we should engage in moral activity at all, unless we recognize human beings as end in themselves and not just means to our own ends.

9

## Some Issues to Consider

- Kant argues that an action's moral worth lies in the maxim, or rule of conduct, on which it is based, not in its consequences; but should we consider consequences when we are deciding on a course of action? In fact, consequences often do feature in moral decisions.

- Kant maintains that moral principles should not be based on empirical factors, such as the contingent conditions of humanity, which would exclude basing moral principles on human needs. But although (some) human needs vary and change, there also seem to be basic, common and permanent human needs, while a lot of moral decision-making does concern these needs and how to meet them.

- Kant acknowledges that all human beings seek happiness, but argues that, as happiness is an indeterminate concept, any attempt to base morality on (achieving) happiness is bound to fail. This is a serious objection to utilitarianism.

- Kant seems to regard actions that are contrary to our desires and inclinations as having greater moral worth than those that are in line with them. But this means that the charitable acts of a cold-hearted philanthropist have greater moral worth than those of a philanthropist who delights in helping others.

- Kant argues that moral laws are expressed as commands. Imperatives are needed because human desires and inclinations may be at odds with moral laws. Only divine or holy beings, whose wills are at one with the moral law, would not require imperatives.

- According to Kant's first formulation of the categorical imperative, moral principles apply universally. If a maxim cannot function as a universal moral law, it should be rejected.

- Would there be any point in having moral principles, or in trying to behave morally, if we did not regard human beings as ends in themselves?
- Is Kant right to argue that morality is independent even of the will of God?
- Kant regards freedom as essential to morality. In order to have wills that are their own, and to be able to adopt as maxims universal principles, to which they hold themselves subject, rational beings must be free. However, he accepts that we cannot prove that we are free.

## Suggestions for Further Reading

Immanuel Kant, *Critique of Practical Reason*, ed. M. Gregor, Cambridge: Cambridge University Press, 1997.

Immanuel Kant, *Critique of Pure Reason*, ed. V. Politis, London: Everyman, 1993.

Immanuel Kant, *Groundwork of the Metaphysics of Morals*, ed. M. Gregor, Cambridge: Cambridge University Press, 1998.

Immanuel Kant, *Prolegomena to Any Future Metaphysic*, ed. B. Logan, London: Routledge, 1996.

Immanuel Kant, *Religion within the Boundaries of Mere Reason*, eds A. Wood & G. di Giovanni, Cambridge: Cambridge University Press, 1998.

E. Cassirer, *Kant's Life and Thought*, trans. J. Haden, New Haven, CT: Yale University Press, 1981.

R. M. Hare, *The Language of Morals*, Oxford and New York: Oxford University Press, 1952.

J. S. Mill, *Utilitarianism*, ed. G. Sher, 2nd edn, Indianapolis/ Cambridge: Hackett Publishing Company, 2001.

H. J. Paton, *The Categorical Imperative*, Philadelphia: University of Pennsylvania Press, 1971.

R. J. Sullivan, *Immanuel Kant's Moral Theory*, Cambridge: Cambridge University Press, 1989.

G. Thomson, *On Kant*, revd edn, Belmont, CA: Wadsworth/ Thomson Learning, 2002.

# Detailed Summary of Kant's *Groundwork of the Metaphysics of Morals*

## Preface (pp. 1–6)

All '**rational** cognition' is either '*material*', concerned with objects, or '*formal*', concerned with '**reason** itself' and the 'universal rules of thinking in general' (p. 1). While the latter is **logic**, the former, concerned with 'objects and the **laws** to which they are subject', is divided into two: **physics** ('**laws of nature**') and **ethics** ('laws of **freedom**') (p. 1). Logic has 'no **empirical** part', as the 'laws of thinking' cannot be drawn from '**experience**' (p. 1). But the other two do, as the former determines 'laws of nature as an object of experience'; the latter, 'laws of the **human being**'s **will**', as **nature** affects it (p. 1). Thus, the first concerns laws of how things happen; the second, laws of how they '**ought** to happen' (p. 1). **Philosophy** based on experience is empirical, but to the extent that its 'teachings' derive from '**a priori** principles', it is '*pure* philosophy' (p. 1). If the latter is 'merely formal', it is '*logic*'; if limited to '**determinate** objects of the understanding', it is '*metaphysics*' (p. 1).

Thus, we have 'a twofold metaphysics': '*of nature*' and '*of morals*' (pp. 1–2). Physics has both an empirical and a rational part, and so does ethics: the former is '***practical anthropology***' and the latter, '*morals*' (p. 2). With both, it is important to keep these parts separate. A **metaphysics of morals** comes before practical anthropology, and all empirical elements must be removed from the metaphysics. The necessity for such a 'pure **moral philosophy**' is clear from 'the common idea of **duty** and **moral laws**' (p. 2). If a law is to be a ground of **moral obligation**, it must have '**absolute necessity**' (p. 2). This 'ground of **obligation**' must not be sought in **human nature**, or the world, but 'in **concepts** of **pure reason**', so it will hold for all **rational beings**, not just human beings (p. 3). Otherwise, although it may be a '**practical rule**', it will not be a 'moral law' (p. 3).

A metaphysics of morals is all the more important, because morals can be corrupted if we know nothing of the '**supreme norm** by which to appraise them correctly' (p. 3). With 'what is to be **morally good**', **conformity** with the moral law is insufficient; it must be done '*for the sake of the law*' (p. 3). Here, we are breaking new ground, as we are concerned with a will of a 'special kind', which would be 'completely determined from a priori principles without any empirical motives' (p. 4). The metaphysics of morals must examine 'the idea and principles of a possible pure will' (p. 4). A distinction needs to be drawn between 'properly moral', *a priori* motives and 'empirical' ones, which the understanding elevates to 'universal concepts merely by comparing experiences' (p. 4). If this is not done, the concept of '*obligation*' will be 'anything but moral' (p. 4). This 'groundwork' is the 'search for and establishment of the *supreme principle of morality*' (p. 5).

## Section I (pp. 7–18)
## Transition from Common Rational to
## Philosophical Moral Cognition

Only a '**good will**' is 'good without limitation' (p. 7). Wit or courage, for example, are 'good and desirable for many purposes', but can be 'harmful', if not used by a good will. Wealth and power can lead to 'arrogance', while 'moderation' and 'self-control' are 'conducive' to a good will, but are not themselves 'good without limitation' (pp. 7–8). A good will is not good because of 'what it effects', but because of its '**volition**' (p. 8). Even if prevented from carrying out any of its purposes, it would still 'shine by itself' (p. 8). This strange idea needs to be tested. We take it that an 'organized being' will contain only the 'most appropriate' **means** to a given **end** (p. 8). Now, if the 'proper end' for a being with 'reason and will' were '*happiness*', nature should not have chosen 'reason' to achieve it, as '**instinct**' would have been better (p. 9).

Indeed, the more reason is concerned with achieving happiness, the further one moves from it, leading some people to hate reason, because of the problems their efforts bring. They envy ordinary people, who are guided by instinct and are relatively uninfluenced by reason. In fact, reason directs us to a worthier purpose than happiness: producing a 'will that is good', not '*as a means*' to other things, but '*in itself*' (p. 10). Reason is necessary for achieving this 'first and **unconditional** purpose' (p. 10). Such a will need not be 'the sole and complete good', but it is the 'highest' one, and the condition of all others, including happiness (p. 10). But 'cultivation of reason', essential to this purpose, does limit 'attainment of the second' good, happiness, which is 'always conditional' (p. 10).

Let us clarify this concept of a good will, by considering 'the concept of **duty**' (p. 10). Actions, regarded as 'contrary to

15

duty', will be ignored, because the question of their being done *'from duty'* does not arise (p. 10). So will those that conform to duty, but which humans perform, despite lack of **inclination**, because it is easy to distinguish those done out of duty from those done for 'self-seeking' reasons (p. 11). It is harder to make this distinction with actions that conform to duty, but which a **person** is inclined to do. For example, it conforms with duty for a shopkeeper not to overcharge his customers, but does he do so from duty? His conduct is **prudent**, so his honesty may arise from **'self-interest'** (p. 11). It is a duty and an 'immediate inclination' to 'preserve one's life', but people's care of it, while conforming with duty, may not arise from it (p. 11). However, where troubles have removed a person's desire to live, his preservation of his life does come from duty, so the **maxim** by which he acts 'has moral content' (p. 11). It is a duty to be 'beneficent', and some people delight in helping others; but such actions, done from inclination, lack 'true **moral worth**' (p. 11). However, if a grief-stricken **philanthropist**, lacking 'all sympathy' with others, still helps them, his action has 'genuine moral worth' (pp. 11–12). This would also be the case with a philanthropist who was, by nature, 'cold and indifferent to the sufferings of others' (p. 12).

People are strongly inclined to happiness, but pursuit of it 'infringes upon some inclinations', and we cannot form a 'determinate' concept of the 'sum of satisfaction of all inclinations under the name of happiness' (p. 12). But, trying to ensure one's happiness is a duty, as lack of it can be a *'temptation to transgression of duty'*. So, promoting happiness from duty, not inclination, has 'moral worth' (p. 12). This is how we should understand biblical passages about loving our neighbour and even our enemy (pp. 12–13). Love, an inclination, cannot be commanded, but **'beneficence** from duty', which 'lies in the will', not feeling, can be (p. 13).

## Section I (pp. 7–18)

The moral worth of an action, done from duty, lies not in what it achieves, but in 'the maxim' upon which it is decided (p. 13). It lies in the *'principle of the will'*, without consideration of 'the ends' that can be achieved (p. 13). Further, *'duty is the necessity of an action from respect for law'* (p. 13). I can have an inclination for the **effect** of my proposed action, but, because it is not 'an activity of a will', no respect for it (p. 13). The only 'object of respect', and so a command, is that which is 'connected with my will' as a 'ground', not an 'effect', and which 'excludes' my inclination (p. 13). An action, done from duty, by setting aside 'the influence of inclination', leaves nothing that could determine the will except law (pp. 13–14). An action's 'moral worth' does not come from its expected effects, because they could have been achieved by 'other causes' (p. 14). Only the *'representation of the law'*, which occurs only in rational beings, in so far as it is the 'determining ground of the will', can be 'the preeminent good we call moral' (p. 14).

But what sort of law is it that must determine the will without consideration of effects, for 'the will to be called good absolutely'? (p. 14). It can only be actions conforming with **'universal law'** as such (p. 14). So, *'I ought never to act except in such a way that I could also will that my maxim should become a universal law'* (pp. 14–15). For example, if in difficulty, may I make a promise without intending to keep it? Is such a course of action 'prudent'? Does it conform with duty to promise falsely? (p. 15). Such promises may cause future 'inconvenience', through loss of confidence in my word, so it might be prudent to abide by the 'general maxim' of only making promises I intend to keep. But this maxim is based on **consequences**, which is not the same as being truthful from duty. Does a lying promise conform with duty? Could it become 'a universal law'? (p. 15). A universal law to lie would end all promises, as it would be pointless to make them. If my maxim became one, it would 'destroy itself' (p. 15).

A maxim, which cannot become a universal law, 'is to be repudiated', not because of any disadvantages it may cause, but because it 'cannot fit as a principle into a possible giving of universal law' (p. 16). What constitutes duty is 'the necessity of my action from *pure* respect for the **practical law**', which is 'the condition of a will **good** *in itself*' (p. 16). In fact, when addressing specific moral questions, people know how to distinguish between good and evil, and what is or is not 'in conformity with duty' (p. 16). **Common human reason** is as likely to be right as any '**philosopher**', who may 'confuse his judgment' with irrelevant considerations (p. 17). Should we, then, exclude philosophy from this whole subject?

The problem is that 'innocence' is 'easily seduced' (p. 17). Human beings experience within themselves 'a powerful counterweight to all the commands of duty': their inclinations, satisfaction of which they sum up as happiness (p. 17). But reason 'issues its **precepts** unremittingly', without concessions to the inclinations (p. 17). So, there is a tendency to 'rationalize against those strict laws of duty', and adapt them to the inclinations (pp. 17–18). Thus, *'common human reason'* is forced to enter 'the field of *practical philosophy*', in order to obtain information about 'the source' of the moral law and how to distinguish it from 'maxims based on need and inclination' (p. 18).

## Section II (pp. 19–51)
## Transition from Popular Moral Philosophy to Metaphysics of Morals

We have not treated our 'concept of duty' as 'a concept of experience', but a common complaint concerns the lack of clear examples of 'the disposition to act from pure duty', lead-ing to doubt about whether actions, which conform with duty, are done *'from duty'* (p. 19). There are also philosophers, who accept our 'concept of **morality**', but claim that human nature is 'too weak' to follow it, and that reason, which should issue law, merely takes care of the inclinations, and tries to ensure their 'compatibility' (p. 19).

Well, experience does not offer a clear example of the maxim of an action conforming with duty and resting 'simply on moral grounds' (p. 19). Only duty seems strong enough to account for some good actions, but other possible motives cannot be excluded. Love of **humanity** leads me to accept that most actions do conform with duty, but close examination often reveals 'the dear self' as their source (p. 20). But, even if no action has ever arisen strictly from duty, this is what reason decrees 'ought to happen' (p. 20). Duty lies 'in the idea of a reason determining the will by means of a priori grounds' (p. 20). This moral law applies, not only to humans, but to 'all *rational beings'*; we would not be entitled to make a precept that was 'valid only under the **contingent conditions of humanity**' into a 'universal precept for every rational nature' (pp. 20–1).

Morality cannot be based on examples, because they need to be 'appraised in accordance with principles of morality' (p. 21). The '**Holy One of the Gospel**' asked people why they called him good, when only **God**, the 'archetype of the good', is so (p. 21). But it is our *'idea* of moral perfection', framed 'a priori' by reason, and connected 'inseparably with the concept of a free will', which gives us our concept of God as 'the high-est good' (p. 21). Examples can illustrate the 'practicability' of the moral law, but they do not enable us to put aside the 'true original', which lies in reason (p. 21).

If the 'supreme basic principle of morality' rests only on

'pure reason', it seems unnecessary to ask whether it is desirable to expound it (p. 21). But there is more interest in 'popular practical philosophy' than in the 'metaphysics of morals' (p. 21). Now, there is nothing wrong with making morality accessible, but 'ascent to the principles of pure reason' needs to come first: otherwise, we get 'half-rationalized principles' (pp. 21–2). Indeed, popular **moralists** often fail to ask whether **moral principles** are to be found in knowledge of human nature or in 'pure rational concepts' (p. 22). A metaphysics of morals, unmixed with theology or anything else, enables us to understand our duties, and also helps us to carry them out. The 'pure thought' of duty and the moral law strongly influences 'the human heart', whereas a 'mixed doctrine of morals', made up of 'inclination' and 'rational concepts', may result in good, but often does not (pp. 22–3).

To sum up, 'all moral concepts' originate 'a priori in reason', and not just in 'speculative' reason'; they cannot be inferred from any 'empirical' knowledge; it is the 'purity of their origin' that enables them to be 'supreme practical principles'; adding empirical elements to them detracts from 'their genuine influence'; it is 'of practical', as well as 'theoretical', importance to draw moral 'concepts and laws from pure reason', and to 'determine the entire faculty of pure **practical reason**'; and, as moral laws apply to all rational beings, their principles must be based, not on 'the special nature of human reason', but on 'the universal concept of a rational being' (p. 23).

In nature, everything 'works in accordance with laws', and only rational beings have 'a *will*' and the ability to 'act *in accordance with the representation* of laws, that is, in accordance with principles' (p. 24). As '*reason*' is needed to derive 'actions from laws, the will is the 'practical reason' (p. 24). If an individual's will is determined by reason, the actions that are understood to be 'objectively necessary are also subjectively necessary', and the will is able to chose, 'independently of inclination', what reason judges to be 'practically necessary' or good (p. 24). Often, however, the human will does not completely conform with reason, and so is not 'thoroughly good' (p. 24). In these cases, although 'objective laws' are presented to the will as 'grounds of reason', the will does not necessarily obey them (p. 24).

An 'objective principle', presented to the will, is a 'command (of reason)', and takes the form of 'an **imperative**' (p. 24). These, expressed by 'an *ought*', indicate the relationship of 'an objective law of reason to a will that by its subjective constitution is not necessarily determined by it' (p. 24). The imperatives state that something is good, but to a will that is not always prepared to do something just because it is 'represented' as good (pp. 24–5). A 'perfectly good will' would 'stand under objective laws (of the good)', but it would not need to be '*necessitated*' to obey the moral law, because it can be determined only by 'the good' (p. 25). Thus, 'the ***divine* will**' and 'a ***holy* will**' do not require imperatives, because their 'volition' already accords with the moral law (p. 25).

Imperatives give commands 'either *hypothetically* or **categorically**' (p. 25). The former indicates the 'practical necessity' of a possible action as a means to a particular end; the latter an action that is 'objectively necessary of itself', without reference to an end (p. 25). In science, there are 'imperatives of **skill**', telling us how to achieve ends by solving specific problems, irrespective of whether or not 'the end is rational and good' (p. 26). The 'precepts' of a physician, trying to heal his patient, and of a poisoner, trying to kill his victim, are of 'equal worth' in relation to achievement of their respective purposes (p. 26). Parents try to ensure that children acquire a range of skills as 'means to all sorts of *discretionary* ends', as they do not know what their future purposes will be (p. 26). Indeed, this 'concern is so great' that they often fail to teach their children about 'the worth of the things that they might make their ends' (p. 26).

All rational beings have one purpose 'by a natural necessity': happiness (p. 26). The **hypothetical imperative**, representing 'the practical necessity of an action as a means to the promotion of happiness, is not a means to a possible purpose (p. 26). But it is one that can be assumed 'a priori in the case of every human being', as it belongs to their 'essence'; and skill in choosing our own 'greatest well-being' is called '*prudence*' (pp. 26–7). However, the 'precept of prudence' is a hypothetical imperative, because it does not command action 'absolutely', but only as a 'means to another purpose' (p. 27). Finally, there is an imperative that does not have 'any other purpose' as its condition (p. 27). This **'categorical' imperative**, or 'imperative of morality', is not concerned with an action's results, but with 'the principle from which the action' follows; what is 'essentially good' in the action is the 'disposition', not the result (p. 27).

Given these three different types of principle, we can speak of '*rules* of skill', where the imperative is '*technical* (belonging to art)'; '*counsels* of prudence', where the imperative is 'pragmatic (belonging to welfare)'; and '*commands* (*laws*) of morality', where the imperative is 'moral (belonging to free conduct as such, that is, to morals)' (p. 27). Only law involves 'the concept of an *unconditional* and objective and hence universally valid *necessity*', which must be obeyed, 'even against inclination' (p. 27). '*Giving counsel*' involves necessity, but under 'subjective and **contingent**' conditions, because different people include different things in their idea of happiness (p. 27).

## Section II (pp. 19–51)

How are imperatives possible? With an 'imperative of skill', the matter is straightforward, but 'imperatives of prudence' are difficult, because 'happiness is such an indeterminate concept' (p. 28). All human beings wish for it, but cannot say exactly what they wish for. This is because the 'concept of happiness' comprises empirical elements, requiring 'a maximum' of present and future well-being (p. 28). A person wills riches, but they bring 'anxiety, envy and intrigue'; another wills knowledge, but this reveals problems of which he was unaware (pp. 28–9). There is no principle by which to determine precisely what would make a person 'truly happy' (p. 29). Yes, he can follow 'empirical counsels' of, for example, 'frugality' and 'courtesy', shown by experience to promote well-being. However, they are not 'commands', because of the insoluble problem of deciding 'which action would promote the happiness of a rational being' (p. 29).

The question of the possibility of the 'imperative of *morality*' is the one that needs solving, because it is not hypothetical (p. 29). But we must bear in mind that no example can show whether there is such an imperative. Imperatives that seem categorical may turn out to be hypothetical. Someone might be told not to promise falsely, but this could be to avoid damaging his reputation. One cannot show that his will is 'determined merely through law' (pp. 29–30). We need to 'investigate entirely a priori the possibility of a *categorical* imperative', as its reality is not given in experience (p. 30). But we can see that only the categorical imperative, which commands unconditionally, 'has the tenor of a practical **law**', because other imperatives concern 'discretionary' purposes (p. 30). When I think of a '*hypothetical* imperative', I do not know what it will contain until I am given the condition; but I know immediately that, apart from the law, a categorical imperative contains 'only the necessity that the maxim be in conformity with this law, while the law contains no condition to which it would be limited' (p. 31). Thus, 'nothing is left with which the maxim of action is to conform but the universality of a law as such' (p. 31). There is only one categorical imperative: *'act only in accordance with that maxim through which you can at the same time will that it become a universal law'* (p. 31). This 'universal imperative' can also be expressed as: *'act as if the maxim of your action were to become by your will a* **universal law of nature**' (p. 31).

Let us consider some examples of duties to ourselves and others. Someone's problems have made him desperate, but he still asks whether duty prevents him taking his life. His maxim is that he should, from self-love, shorten his life when its troubles outweigh its 'agreeableness' (pp. 31–2). Could this become a 'universal law of nature'? (p. 32). There is a clear **contradiction** in a nature whose law would be to use the same feeling that impels 'towards the furtherance of life' as the means of destroying it (p. 32). This maxim opposes 'the supreme principle of all duty', and could not be a universal law of nature (p. 32). A person needs to borrow money, but, though unable to do so, must promise to repay it within a specified time. His conscience prompts him to ask whether this would be 'contrary to duty' (p. 32). If he does so, his maxim will be: if I need money, I shall borrow it, and promise repayment, even though I cannot do so. Could this be a universal law? No, the maxim would make promises and the expectations of them impossible, as no one would believe them.

A man has a talent, capable of cultivation into general usefulness, but 'comfortable circumstances' make doing so seem like too much trouble (p. 32). Is it consistent with duty to neglect his talents? He cannot will this as a universal law, because, as a 'rational being', he 'necessarily wills' development of all his capacities, since they serve him and have many uses (p. 33). Another is prospering, but sees others faring badly. He feels inclined to care only for himself, neither asking for, nor giving, help. If this maxim were a universal law, the human race would survive, but it is impossible to will it as a 'law of nature', because such a will would conflict with itself (p. 33). There are occasions when one needs others' love and sympathy, but this law would remove any possibility of help.

There are some actions that cannot 'even be *thought* without contradiction as a universal law'; with others, there is no 'inner impossibility', but we cannot will their maxim as a universal law, because 'such a will would contradict itself' (p. 33). Sometimes, when not fulfilling a duty, we discover 'a contradiction in our own will': we do not will that the maxim of our action become a universal law, but the opposite of it. However, we try to make an exception of ourselves, to suit 'our inclination' (p. 34). This is a case of inclination resisting the 'precept of reason', but we still recognize the 'validity of the categorical imperative' (p. 34).

We have shown that, if duty is to legislate for our actions, it 'can be expressed only in categorical imperatives', but we have not proved *a priori* that such an imperative exists (p. 34). We must not think that we shall find it in some special quality of human nature. Duty must 'hold for all rational beings', and human nature cannot give us 'an objective principle', upon which we would be '*directed* to act' against our inclinations (p. 34). Anything 'empirical' is 'highly prejudicial to the purity of morals', which requires the **principle of action** to be free of empirical elements (pp. 34–5).

So, is it a 'necessary law' for all rational beings to 'appraise their actions in accordance with such maxims as they themselves could will to serve as universal laws'? (p. 35). If there is such a law, it must be connected *a priori* with 'the concept of the will of a rational being as such' (p. 35). Here we are concerned with a subject that belongs to the 'metaphysics of morals': the 'relation of the will to itself in so far as it determines itself only by reason' (p. 36). This means that there can be no empirical element, because, if reason alone determines conduct, 'it must necessarily do so a priori' (p. 36).

The 'objective ground' of the will's **self-determination** is an end (p. 36). The ends that a rational being takes as *'effects* of his actions' are relative, because their only worth is in relation to that being's particular **desires** (p. 36). Such relative ends provide 'no universal principles, no principles valid and necessary for all rational beings' (p. 36). But what if there was something which, *'as an end in itself'*, has **'absolute worth'**? (p. 36). This alone would be the 'ground of a possible categorical imperative' (p. 36). Human, and all rational, beings exist as ends in themselves, and, in all they do, whether to themselves or others, must always be regarded as ends. This is why, unlike beings 'without reason', which have only 'relative worth, as means', they 'are called *persons*' (p. 37). And they are not 'subjective ends', with merely a 'worth *for us*', but '*objective ends*' (p. 37). Without them, 'nothing of *absolute worth* would be found anywhere' (p. 37).

If there is to be a 'supreme practical principle' (and, in relation to the human will, a 'categorical imperative'), it must, as 'an *objective* principle of the will', relate to that which is 'necessarily an end for everyone because it is an *end in itself*' (p. 37). The ground of this principle is: *'rational nature exists as an end in itself'* (p. 37). Of course, human beings represent their own existence in this way, but so do all rational beings, on 'the same rational ground' (p. 37). Thus, it is an *'objective* principle', from which 'as a supreme practical ground, it must be possible to derive all laws of the will' (pp. 37–8). This gives the 'practical imperative': '*So act that you use humanity, whether in your own person or in the person of any other, always at the same time as an end, never merely as a means*' (p. 38).

Does this work? Let us go back to the examples. With the 'concept of necessary duty to oneself', someone contemplating suicide will question the consistency of his action 'with the idea of humanity *as an end in itself*' (p. 38). By killing himself, he would use his person as a means to maintaining a 'tolerable condition up to the end of life' (p. 38). But, as a human being, who must be regarded as 'an end in itself', he cannot dispose of himself in this way (p. 38). As far as 'necessary duty to others' is concerned, someone promising falsely uses another human being '*merely as a means*' (p. 38). This is true of any 'assaults on the freedom and property of others' (p. 38). Someone, violating 'the rights of human beings', shows that they do not value them as ends (p. 38). With 'contingent (meritorious) duty to oneself', action must also '*harmonize*' with the principle of treating 'humanity in our person as an end in itself' (pp. 38–9). Human beings have 'predispositions to greater perfection'; neglecting them may comply with '*preservation* of humanity as an end in itself but not with *furtherance* of this end' (p. 39). Turning to 'meritorious duty to others', all human beings have happiness as their natural end (p. 39). Humanity might survive if no one added to others' happiness, as long as they did not subtract from it. But this would be only 'negative' agreement with the principle of '*humanity as an end in itself*': as far as possible, the ends of those who are ends in themselves must also be mine (p. 39).

This principle that human and other rational beings are ends in themselves cannot come from experience. This is because it is universal, applying to all rational beings, about whom experience tells us nothing; and because it does not represent human beings as having been made an end by human beings themselves, but as 'an objective end', which 'ought as law to constitute the supreme limiting condition of all subjective ends' (p. 39). Thus, it arises from 'pure reason' (p. 39). All practical **lawgiving** is grounded *'objectively in the rule* and the form of universality', which fits it to be a law (p. 39). Subjectively, its ground is 'the *end*', but, as 'the subject of all ends is every rational being as an end in itself', this gives us the idea of *'the will of every rational being as a will giving universal law'* (p. 39). The will is subject to the law in such a way that it must be seen 'as also giving the law to itself'. Thus, the will is subject to the law, a law that it gives to itself (p. 39).

The earlier discussion of imperatives excluded any element of **interest** as an incentive, through the assumption that they are categorical, but the existence of categorical imperatives could not be proved. However, 'some determination' of the imperative itself could indicate 'renunciation of all interest' as the feature that distinguishes categorical from hypothetical imperatives, and this is done through the 'idea of the will of every rational being as a *will giving universal law'* (p. 40). A will that *'stands under law'* may be tied to it by interest, but, if the will itself is the 'supreme lawgiver', it cannot depend on interest (p. 40). A categorical imperative commands that everything be done from the maxim of one's will as one that 'could at the same time have as its object itself as giving universal law' (p. 40). Thus, 'the practical principle, and the imperative the will obeys', is unconditional, not being based on interest (p. 40).

It is no surprise that previous efforts to identify 'the principle of morality' failed (p. 40). It was recognized that the human being is bound to duty by law, but not that 'he is subject *only to laws given by himself but still universal*', which we call **'autonomy of the will'** (p. 40). This is different from just being bound by law. With law that does not flow from the human being's will, *'something else'* has to get him to obey it (pp. 40–1). One did not have a duty, only an action made necessary by 'a certain interest', which is **'heteronomy'** of the will; and, as the imperative was always conditional, it was not a 'moral command' (p. 41).

All rational beings seeing themselves as giving universal law through the maxims of their will gives rise to the concept '*of a **kingdom of ends**'* (p. 41). All rational beings must treat themselves and others as ends, not means. They are lawgiving members of the kingdom of ends, but also subject to its laws. Morality consists in referring 'all action to the lawgiving by which alone a kingdom of ends is possible', which must arise from the will of all rational beings (p. 42). Its principle is to do no action unless the will can regard itself as *'giving universal law through its maxim'* (p. 42). If the maxims are not in accord with this principle, acting in accordance with it is *'duty'*, which depends, not on 'inclinations', but on 'the relation of all rational beings to one another' (p. 42).

Only under morality can a rational being be *'an end in itself'*, because only through morality can he be a 'lawgiving member in the kingdom of ends' (p. 42). Only morality, and human beings, in so far as they are capable if it, have dignity. Such qualities as wit and humour are valuable, but 'fidelity in promises and benevolence' have **inner worth** (p. 42). This comes, not from their effects, but from dispositions 'in maxims of the will that in this way are ready to manifest themselves through actions', even if they achieve nothing (p. 43). And why is this? It is because of the '*share* it affords a rational being *in the giving of universal laws*', which equips him to be 'a member of a possible kingdom of ends' (p. 43). His nature, as an end in itself, destines him to be so, and, as a lawgiver in the kingdom of ends, he is 'free with respect to all laws of nature, obeying only those which he himself gives and in accordance with which his maxims can belong to a giving of universal law' (p. 43). Indeed, autonomy is 'the ground of the dignity of human nature and of every rational creature' (p. 43).

In fact, these three ways of 'representing the principle of morality' are all 'formulae of the very same law' (p. 43). All maxims have 'a *form*', universality, so the 'formula of the moral imperative' is expressed in a way which shows that maxims must be chosen 'as if they were to hold as universal laws of nature' (p. 43). They have 'a *matter*' or end, and the formula states that, in every maxim, 'a rational being', as 'an end in itself', must be 'the limiting condition of all merely relative and arbitrary ends' (pp. 43–4). And the formula must provide '*a complete determination* of all maxims', so 'all maxims from one's own lawgiving are to harmonize with a possible king-dom of ends as with a kingdom of nature' (p. 44). So, an '*absolutely good*' will is one that 'cannot be evil', and thus one 'whose maxim, if made universal law, can never conflict with itself' (p. 44). The 'sole condition' under which there can be no such conflict is to 'act always on that maxim whose universality as a law you can at the same time will' (p. 44). This is a categorical imperative, which can be expressed as: '*act in accordance with maxims that can at the same time have as their object themselves as universal laws of nature*' (p. 44).

Setting itself an end is what distinguishes rational nature from 'the rest of nature' (p. 44). However, the idea of an absolutely good will requires '**abstraction**' from 'every end to be *effected*', which would make every will 'only relatively good' (p. 44). So, the end must be thought of as existing

independently, and, because a good will cannot be 'subordinated to any other object', as 'nothing other than the subject
of all possible ends itself' (pp. 44–5). The principle of acting
towards rational beings (including yourself) so that 'in your
maxim it holds at the same time as an end in itself' is the same
as the 'basic principle' of acting on a maxim which 'contains
in itself its own universal validity for every rational being':
the rational being is 'the basis of all maxims of actions, never
merely as a means but as the supreme limiting condition in
the use of all means' (p. 45).

As 'an end in itself', every rational being must, in relation
to any law to which he is subject, be able to see himself as a
giver of universal laws, because it is the 'fitness of his maxims
for giving universal law' that identifies him as an end in himself; and this 'dignity' that he possesses over 'merely **natural
beings**' means that he must adopt maxims on the basis that
he and other rational beings are lawgivers, or persons (p. 45).
This makes possible a 'world of rational beings . . . as a kingdom of ends': all persons, as members, give their own laws
(p. 45). The 'formal principle' of the maxims of these lawgiving persons is: 'act as if your maxims were to serve . . . as a
universal law (for all rational beings)' (p. 45). A kingdom of
ends is possible only through maxims 'imposed upon oneself', and would be created 'through maxims whose rule the
categorical imperative prescribes to all rational beings *if they
were universally followed*' (p. 45). A rational being may himself
adhere to this maxim, but there is no guarantee that others
will, or that the kingdom of nature will 'harmonize with him'
towards creating a kingdoms of ends (which his own adher-
ence to this maxim makes possible), and thus promote his
happiness (p. 46). Nevertheless, the law of acting 'in accordance with the maxims of a member giving universal laws for

a merely possible kingdom of ends' still 'commands categorically' (p. 46). But it is in the 'independence of maxims' from any advantage that might be achieved by following them that their '**sublimity**' lies; and also 'the worthiness of every rational subject to be a lawgiving member in the kingdom of ends' (p. 46). Even if the kingdom of ends became a reality not an idea, and was 'united under one sovereign' with the kingdom of nature, this would not increase its 'inner worth' (p. 46). Its 'sole absolute lawgiver' would still have to appraise 'the worth of rational beings only by their disinterested conduct, prescribed to themselves merely from that idea' (p. 46). '*Morality*' is 'the relation of actions to the autonomy of the will' (p. 46). A '*permitted*' action is one that can coexist with the autonomy of the will, while a 'forbidden' one cannot (p. 46). The maxims of a '*holy*', or 'absolutely good', will 'necessarily harmonize with the laws of autonomy' (p. 46). '*Obligation*' arises when a will that is 'not absolutely good' depends on the '**principle of autonomy**'; '*duty*' is the 'objective necessity of an action from obligation' (p. 46).

When we think of duty, we think of being subject to the law, but also see 'a certain sublimity and *dignity*' in one who carries out his duties (p. 46). There is no sublimity in being subject to the moral law, but there is in being '*lawgiving*' in relation to it and in being subject to it for that reason alone (p. 46). Respect for the law gives actions their 'moral worth', and humanity's dignity 'consists just in this capacity to give universal law, though with the condition of also being itself subject to this very lawgiving' (pp. 46–7).

## Autonomy of the Will as the Supreme Principle of Morality (p. 47)

Its autonomy is the property of the will 'by which it is a law to itself'; and the 'principle of autonomy' is so to choose maxims that they are 'also included as a universal law in the same volition' (p. 47). This 'practical rule' is an imperative, but, as this is a **'synthetic proposition'** (albeit one which 'must be capable of being **cognized** completely a priori'), it cannot be proved **analytically** (p. 47). However it is 'the sole principle of morals' (p. 47).

## Heteronomy of the Will as the Source of All Spurious Principles of Morality (pp. 47–8)

Heteronomy is the result of the will seeking its determining law *'anywhere else* than in the fitness of its maxims for its own giving of universal law' (p. 47). When this happens, only hypothetical, not categorical, imperatives are possible. For example, I will say I ought not to lie to keep my reputation, rather than I ought not to lie, despite there being no ill consequences. The categorical imperative must 'abstract from all objects', so that they do not influence the will (p. 48). Thus, I ought to promote the happiness of others, not through inclination or because it matters to me, but because 'a maxim that excludes this cannot be included as a universal law in one and the same volition' (p. 48).

## *Division* of All Possible Principles of Morality Taken from Heteronomy Assumed as the Basic Concept *(pp. 48–51)*

All such principles will be either *'empirical* or *rational'* (p. 48). The former are unsuitable as a ground for moral laws, because the universality of the application of moral laws to 'all rational beings' falls if they are based on the *'special constitution of human nature'* or its 'contingent circumstances' (p. 48). Those based on *'one's own happiness'* are particularly 'objectionable', as they place the 'motives to virtue and those to vice in one class and only teach us to calculate better', while eliminating specific differences between them (pp. 48–9). The 'special sense' of '**moral feeling**', which some claim to possess, is closer to morality, because it does show 'esteem' for 'virtue', and not merely a desire for any 'advantage' that may attach to it (p. 49).

Turning to rational grounds, 'the **ontological** concept of *perfection'* is better than the **theological** one, which takes morality from 'a divine, all-perfect will' (p. 49). This is because we cannot know 'the perfection' of the divine will, while the concept that we have of it, apart from morality, which includes ideas of 'power and vengefulness', would suggest a basis for morality which would be 'directly opposed' to it (p. 49). If forced to choose between 'the moral sense and that of perfection generally', I would opt for the latter, because it at least 'preserves the indeterminate idea (of a will good in itself) unfalsified' (pp. 49–50).

There is no need for detailed refutation of these 'doctrines' (p. 50). Whenever 'an **object of the will**' becomes the 'basis for prescribing the rule that determines the will', the result is 'heteronomy' and a **conditional imperative** (p. 50). It does not matter what the object is (it may be one's own happiness), the will is still determined by an incentive: '*I ought to do something on this account, that I will something else*' (p. 50). The result is a law given by nature, which is 'contingent', and so it cannot serve as an '**apodictic**' moral rule (p. 50). In this situation, instead of autonomy of the will, with the will giving itself the law, there would be '*only heteronomy* of the will': the law would be given 'by means of the subject's nature' (p. 50). The 'fitness of the maxims of every good will to make themselves into universal law is itself the sole law that the will of every rational being imposes upon itself, without having to put underneath it some incentive or interest as a basis' (pp. 50–1). The solution of the problem of how '*such a synthetic practical proposition is possible a priori*' is not to be found in the 'metaphysics of morals', but this exploration of the 'generally received concept of morality' shows that its basis is autonomy of the will (p. 51). So, morality requires a 'possible *synthetic use of pure practical reason*', but first we must provide a '*critique* of this rational faculty itself' (p. 51).

## Section III (pp. 52–66)
## Transition from Metaphysics of Morals to the Critique of Pure Practical Reason

### *The Concept of Freedom is the Key to the Explanation of the Autonomy of the Will (pp. 52–3)*

Will is a 'kind of **causality** of living beings in so far as they are rational', while freedom would enable that causality to operate 'independently of alien causes' (p. 52). The concept of causality brings with it that of the law of cause and effect, and freedom is a 'special kind' of causality, which operates according to special 'immutable laws' (p. 52). The freedom or 'autonomy' of the will is 'the will's property of being a law to itself', which points to one principle only: that of acting 'on no other maxim than that which can also have as object itself as a universal law' (p. 52). But this is the 'formula of the categorical imperative'; so, a free will, and one subject to moral laws, are the same thing (pp. 52–3).

### *Freedom Must be Presupposed as a Property of the Will of All Rational Beings (pp. 53–4)*

But it is insufficient to attribute (it cannot be **demonstrated**) freedom of the will to ourselves, based on 'supposed experiences of human nature', since it must apply to all rational beings with a will (p. 53). Indeed, it is impossible to think of 'a reason that would consciously receive direction' from outside itself, since, if it did so, its judgments would be attributable not to 'reason but to an impulse' (p. 54). Every rational being must be free, because his will cannot be his own unless it is free.

### *Of the Interest Attaching to the Ideas of Morality (pp. 54–8)*

We have 'traced the determinate concept of morality back to the idea of freedom' (p. 54). Although it cannot be proved, we must presuppose it, in order to consider a being as 'rational and endowed with consciousness of his causality with respect to actions, that is, with a will' (p. 54). But involved in this idea of freedom is the awareness that we must adopt as maxims those that can 'hold universally as principles', and which, therefore, can 'serve for our own giving of universal laws' (p. 54). But why should I do so, when 'no interest *impels* me'? (p. 54). Indeed, if I did have an interest, there would be no categorical imperative.

In the idea of freedom, we have 'presupposed the moral law,

namely the principle of the autonomy of the will', but we have not proved its reality (p. 55). So, if asked 'why the universal validity of our maxim as a law must be the limiting condition of our actions', and why we attach worth to acting in this way, we have no adequate answer (p. 55). Of course, what would make us worthy to be happy is interesting, but we still do not know why we should freely 'detach ourselves from all empirical interest', and hold ourselves subject to the moral law (p. 55). In fact, we seem to go in circles. We regard ourselves as free, in order to think of ourselves as 'under moral laws', and then as under these laws, because 'we have ascribed to ourselves freedom of will' (p. 55). But there is a way forward: to consider the difference between, on the one hand, thinking of ourselves as 'causes efficient a priori', and, on the other, 'in terms of our actions as effects' (p. 56).

It requires little intelligence to see that 'all representations which come to us involuntarily', such as those of the **senses**, enable us to know objects only as they affect us. We do not know what they are in themselves: 'we can achieve only cognition *of appearances*, never of **things** *in themselves*' (p. 56). But we do assume that, behind the appearances, the *'world of sense'*, there are things in themselves, the *'world of understanding'* (p. 56). Indeed, human beings cannot even claim to know what they are in themselves through the knowledge that comes from **'inner sensation'** (p. 56). As we obtain our concept of ourselves empirically, not *a priori*, the information comes through 'inner sense', and is 'made up of nothing but appearances' (p. 56). However, behind these, we assume that there is an 'ego' (p. 56). So, as receivers of sensations, we think of ourselves as part of the *'world of sense'*, but, when we have immediate consciousness of things, we think of ourselves as part of the *'intellectual world'* (p. 56).

Human beings have a capacity by which they distinguish themselves from everything else: *'reason'* (p. 57). This 'pure self-activity' stands even 'above the *understanding*', which can only produce concepts that *'bring sensible representations under rules'*. However, reason can distinguish between the worlds of sense and understanding, 'marking out limits for the understanding itself' (p. 57). A rational being must regard himself *'as intelligence'*, and as belonging to 'the world of understanding' (p. 57). Thus, he has 'two standpoints' from which to regard the relationship between himself and laws (p. 57). As part of the world of sense, he is subject to laws of nature, but, as part of the **'intelligible world'**, he is subject to laws that are 'independent of nature', and which are 'grounded merely in reason' (p. 57).

This means that a human being, as a rational being, can only think of the 'causality' of his will 'under the idea of freedom' (p. 57). And bound up with the idea of freedom are 'the concept of *autonomy*' and 'the universal principle of morality' (p. 57). Indeed, the latter is the 'ground of all actions of all *rational beings*, just as the law of nature is the ground of all appearances' (p. 57). So, when we think of ourselves as free, we regard ourselves as members of the world of understanding, with an autonomous will and subject to morality. However, when we think of ourselves as 'put under obligation', we see ourselves as members of the worlds of both sense and understanding (p. 58).

### How is a Categorical Imperative Possible? (pp. 58–9)

A rational being can 'call his causality a *will*' only as a member of 'the world of understanding'; as a member of 'the world of sense', his actions are determined by 'desires and inclinations' (p. 58). However, as the former *'contains the ground'* of the latter and of its laws, he knows himself as 'intelligence', subject to the law of the former, and thus to 'autonomy of the will' (p. 58). He must regard 'the laws of the world of under-standing' as imperatives (p. 58). Categorical imperatives are possible, therefore, because 'the idea of freedom' gives him membership of the world of understanding; and, were he this alone, his actions would always conform with autonomy of the will (p. 58). However, since he also belongs to the world of sense, they *'ought* to be in conformity with it' (p. 58). Now, this 'categorical *ought*' is a 'synthetic proposition a priori', because there is added to my will, which is subject to desires, the idea of that will 'belonging to the world of the understanding' (pp. 58–9).

This is confirmed by 'common human reason' (p. 59). Even a 'hardened scoundrel', faced with instances of honesty and benevolence, would like to apply them in his own life, but is prevented by 'his inclinations and impulses' (p. 59). However, in thought, he frees his will from the 'impulses of sensibil-ity', and is aware of a good will, which 'constitutes the law for his evil will as a member of the world of sense' (p. 59). He acknowledges its 'authority', even though he 'transgresses' it (p. 59).

### On the Extreme Boundary of All Practical Philosophy (pp. 59–66)

All human beings consider themselves as 'having free will', which means that they judge actions as 'being such that they *ought to have been done even though they were not*' (p. 59). How-ever, freedom is 'only an *idea* of reason' (p. 60). Its **objective reality** can be doubted, 'whereas nature is a *concept of the under-*

*standing*', which proves its 'reality in examples from experience' (p. 60). Thus, there is a '**dialectic of reason**' in relation to the will, because the freedom claimed for it seems to contradict 'natural necessity' (p. 60). But, although natural necessity seems more credible than freedom, the later is essential in order for us to use 'reason in our conduct' (p. 60). So, we must assume the absence of any real contradiction between freedom and natural necessity in the 'very same human actions', because we cannot relinquish either one (p. 60). Nevertheless, we shall be unable to understand the possibility of freedom unless we eliminate 'this seeming contradiction' (p. 60).

The contradiction would be inescapable if one, who considers himself free, thinks of himself *in the same sense*' when he considers himself as 'subject to the law of nature with regard to the same action' (p. 60). It is essential for '**speculative philosophy**' to show that the two can 'coexist' (p. 60). The claim to freedom of the will is based on awareness of 'the independence of reason from merely subjectively determining causes' (p. 61). A human being puts himself 'in a relation to determining grounds of an altogether different kind' when he considers himself as 'an intelligence', possessing a 'will' and with 'causality', as opposed to 'a **phenomenon** in the world of sense' (p. 61). He sees that there can be both, and that there is no contradiction in holding that something belonging to the world of sense is subject to laws of which it is independent as a 'being *in itself*' (p. 61). The human being claims to have a will, which makes possible actions that can be performed only by ignoring all desires. He is subject to laws, given by 'pure reason', which 'apply to him immediately and categorically', and, as 'intelligence', he does not allow himself to be influenced by 'inclinations' from the world of sense (p. 62). Of course, we cannot explain *'how freedom is possible'* (p. 62).

It is a 'mere idea, the objective reality of which can in no way be presented in accordance with laws of nature'; nor can it be 'presented in any possible experience' (p. 63). The fact is that where 'determination by laws of nature' ceases, so too does any possibility of explanation (p. 63). However, to those who affirm the impossibility of freedom, who find it hard to think of a human being as 'intelligence', and who maintain that the law of nature alone applies to human actions, we can only say that 'things in themselves (though hidden) must lie behind appearances as their ground' (p. 63).

It is as impossible to explain freedom of the will as to account for undoubted human interest in moral laws. But it is important, if rational beings are going to will 'that for which reason alone prescribes the "ought"', that reason makes fulfilling duty pleasurable, although it is not clear why a mere thought should be able to do so (p. 64). Anyway, it may not be possible to explain why morality interests us, but the moral law is not valid for us, because it interests us; it interests, because 'it is valid for us as human beings' (p. 64).

So, a categorical imperative is possible solely through presupposition of 'the idea of freedom' (p. 64). How freedom itself is possible cannot be 'seen by any human reason', but presupposing it is both '*possible*' and '*necessary*', in order for a rational being, aware of 'his causality through reason and so of a will (which is distinct from desires) to put it under all his voluntary actions as their condition' (p. 65). However, we cannot explain how '*the mere principle of the universal validity of all its maxims as law*' can, in the absence of any other incentive, produce in rational beings 'an interest that would be called purely *moral*' (p. 65). And it would be just as difficult to work out 'how freedom itself as the causality of a will is possible' (p. 65). So, we have reached 'the highest limit of all moral inquiry' (p. 65). And these are important matters to decide, so that reason does not look for 'the supreme motive' of morals in the world of sense, or (which is equally undesirable) try to locate it in '**transcendent concepts**, called the intelligible world, and so lose itself among phantoms' (pp. 65–6). However, the idea of a 'pure world of understanding', even if 'all knowledge stops as its boundary', is valuable (p. 66). It fosters in us a keen interest in the moral law, through the 'ideal of a universal kingdom of *ends in themselves* (rational beings)', of which, by following 'maxims of freedom as if they were laws of nature', we can be members (p. 66).


## Concluding Remarks (p. 66)

Using reason to speculate on nature results in an 'absolute necessity': that of a '**supreme cause of the *world***' (p. 66). So, too, does using practical reason in relation to freedom: that of *'laws of actions* of a rational being as such'. It is an 'essential *principle*' of our reason that it tries to achieve 'consciousness of its *necessity*'; but, it cannot do so except under some *'condition'* (p. 66). Reason is forced just to assume 'the unconditionally necessary', without being able to make it 'comprehensible' (p. 66). So, it is no surprise that reason cannot make 'the 'absolute necessity' of an 'unconditional practical law', like the categorical imperative, comprehensible, because it is not prepared to do so through a condition, such as some 'interest', as this would mean that it was not the moral law, 'the supreme law of freedom' (p. 66). However, we can at least understand the *'incomprehensibility'* of 'the practical unconditional necessity of the moral imperative', which is all that can be expected when we approach the 'very boundary of human reason' (p. 66).

**Overview**

*Preface (pp. 1–6)*

Kant explains that, to be the ground of moral obligation, and to hold for all rational beings, as well as human beings, moral law must have absolute necessity, which can only be found in concepts of pure reason, not in human nature. What is good cannot merely conform with the moral law, but must be done for its sake, so properly moral *a priori* motives need to be distinguished from empirical ones. A metaphysics of morals is important, because, without a supreme norm, against which to test them, morals can be corrupted. The *Groundwork* is about the search for the supreme principle of morality.

*Section I (pp. 7–18)*
*Transition from Common Rational to*
*Philosophical Moral Cognition*

Kant maintains that only a good will, which is good because of its volition (not because of what it accomplishes), is good without limitation. It is good in itself, not as a means to other things. This can be clarified by considering duty and actions that, although they conform to duty, are also in line with a person's inclinations. For example, a shopkeeper's motive for not overcharging his customers might not be duty but the self-interested one of not driving them away. However, the charitable acts of a philanthropist, out of sympathy with humanity, have moral worth, as they are contrary to his inclination. An action's moral worth lies in the maxim upon which it is decided, not in what it accomplishes. An action, done from duty, which excludes inclination, leaves only law to determine the will; and the representation of the law as the determining ground of the will occurs only in rational beings.

For the will to be absolutely good, the only law determining it must be universal law as such: 'I ought never to act except in such a way that I could also will that my maxim should become a universal law.' Kant illustrates his point by examples, including that of a desperate person, who contemplates making a promise without intending to keep it. A maxim of rejecting this course of action, because people might not believe him in future, would be based on consequences, not duty. However, the maxim of making lying promises could not become a universal law, because it would end all promises, and thus destroy itself. A maxim must be rejected if it is unsuitable as a principle for a possible giving of universal law.

In making moral decisions, common human reason is as likely to be right as the philosopher, but philosophy can help to distinguish the moral law from maxims based on inclination.

### Section II (pp. 19–51)
### Transition from Popular Moral Philosophy to Metaphysics of Morals

Kant concedes that experience does not offer a clear example of a maxim conforming with duty and resting simply on moral grounds. However, this is what reason decrees ought to happen: duty lies in the idea of reason determining the will by means of *a priori* grounds. As the moral law applies to all rational beings, a precept, valid only under the contingent conditions of human beings, could not become a universal one. Moral principles, based on human nature, instead of pure rational concepts, result in a confused, and potentially harmful, morality. Moral concepts originate *a priori* in the reason.

44

They cannot be inferred from empirical knowledge, being based, not on the special nature of human beings, but on the universal concept of a rational being.

In nature, everything operates according to laws, but only rational beings possess a will, and the ability to act according to the representation of laws. Reason is needed to derive actions from laws, but the human will often does not conform with reason, disobeying objective laws presented to it by the reason. Thus, an objective moral law is put to human beings in the form of an imperative, expressed by an ought. However, a divine or holy will would not need imperatives, because its volition already accords with the moral law.

Imperatives can command either hypothetically or categorically. The former indicates that an action is necessary as a means to some end; the latter that it is necessary of itself, without referring to an end. Thus, in science there are imperatives of skill, telling us how to achieve ends, irrespective of whether or not the end is good. Again, the precept of prudence, relating to achieving happiness, is a hypothetical imperative: it commands action as a means to another purpose. But the imperative of morality is categorical, as it concerns, not an action's results, but the principle from which it follows. Only moral law involves the concept of an unconditional, objective and universally valid necessity, which must be obeyed against inclination.

But the reality of categorical imperatives is not given in experience, and it is possible that what appear to be categorical imperatives may prove hypothetical. But the difference between them is that, with hypothetical ones, what they contain is not known until the condition is given, whereas a categorical imperative contains only the necessity that the maxim adopted conforms with the moral law. There is only one categorical imperative: 'act only in accordance with that maxim through which you can at the same time will that it become a universal law', which can also be expressed as: 'act as if the maxim of your action were to become by your will a universal law of nature'.

Kant illustrates the point with examples, including that of a person who is doing well, but who sees that others are not. He decides to look after only himself. Humanity would survive the adoption of such a maxim, but it could not be willed as a universal law, because it would conflict with itself, removing all possibility of the help that everybody needs at times. Some actions cannot be thought of as universal laws without contradiction. Others cannot be willed as universal laws because such a will would contradict itself.

The existence of categorical imperatives cannot be proved *a priori*. They will not be found in human nature, because anything empirical is prejudicial to the purity of morals. But, if there is such a thing, it must be connected *a priori* with the concept of the will of a rational being as such: if reason determines conduct, it must do so *a priori*.

The objective ground of the will's self-determination is an end. But the ends that are the effects of a rational being's actions have only relative worth in relation to particular desires, and provide no universal principles. To be the ground of a possible categorical imperative, an end in itself, of absolute worth, is needed. But human and all rational beings are ends in themselves, because without them, there is nothing of absolute worth. And this is an objective principle, from which it is possible to derive all laws of the will, yielding the practical imperative: 'So act that you use humanity, whether in your own person or in the person of any other, always at the same time as an end, never merely as a means.' Kant illustrates this by referring to a previous example: someone who promises falsely uses another human being as a means.

The principle that human and rational beings are ends in themselves does not come from experience, which gives no information about rational beings, but from pure reason. All practical lawgiving is grounded objectively in the rule and form of universality, which fits it to be law. Subjectively, its ground is the end, but the subject of all ends is every rational being as an end in itself. This gives the idea of the will of every rational being as a will giving universal law. And the will is subject to the law in such a way that it must be seen as giving the law to itself.

Although the existence of categorical imperatives cannot be proved, renunciation of interest could be what distinguishes them from hypothetical ones. If a will is itself the supreme lawgiver, it cannot depend on interest. Thus, the imperative the will obeys is unconditional, not being based on inter-est. Human beings are subject only to laws given by them-selves, but still universal, and this is autonomy of the will. It is different from being bound by law, where somebody else has to ensure obedience.

Rational beings seeing themselves as giving universal law through the maxims of their will gives rise to the concept of a kingdom of ends. All rational beings must treat themselves and others as ends, not means, doing no action unless the will can regard itself as giving universal law through its maxim. Giving universal laws equips a rational being for member-ship of a possible kingdom of ends, and, as a lawgiver in the kingdom of ends, he is free with respect to all laws of nature, obeying only those which he himself gives.

An absolutely good will cannot be evil; its maxim can never conflict with itself. The sole condition under which there can be no conflict is always to act on maxims that can be willed as universal laws. This categorical imperative can be expressed as: 'act in accordance with maxims that can at the same time have as their object themselves as universal laws of nature'.

The idea of an absolutely good will requires abstraction from every end to be effected, as these would make the will only relatively good. The end must be thought of as existing independently, and, because a good will cannot be subordinated to any other object, as itself the subject of all possible ends. The rational being is the basis of all maxims of actions, never merely as a means but as the supreme limiting condition in the use of all means.

As ends in themselves, rational beings must see themselves as givers of universal laws, in relation to laws to which they are subject, because it is the fitness of their maxims for giving universal moral law that identifies them as ends in themselves. They must adopt maxims on the basis that they are lawgivers, acting as if their maxims are to serve as a universal law for all rational beings. It is in the independence of their maxims from any advantage that might be achieved by following them that the worthiness of rational beings to be lawgiving members in the kingdom of ends lies.

Morality is the relation of actions to the autonomy of the will. The maxims of a holy will necessarily harmonize with the laws of autonomy. Obligation arises when a will that is not absolutely good depends on the principle of autonomy.

## Autonomy of the Will *as the Supreme Principle of Morality* (p. 47)

Its autonomy is the property of the will by which it is a law to itself. The principle of autonomy is so to choose maxims that they are also included as a universal law in the same volition.

This practical rule is an imperative, and a synthetic proposition (capable of being cognized completely *a priori*), as it cannot be proved analytically. However it is the sole principle of morals.

### Heteronomy of the Will *as the Source of All Spurious Principles of Morality* (pp. 47–8)

Heteronomy results from the will seeking its determining law elsewhere than in the fitness of its maxims for its own giving of universal law. This produces only hypothetical imperatives, as with the maxim of not lying just to keep one's reputation.

### Division *of All Possible Principles of Morality Taken from Heteronomy Assumed as the Basic Concept* (pp. 48–51)

Empirical principles are unsuitable as a ground for moral laws. Universal application of moral laws to all rational beings falls if they are based on contingent circumstances of human nature. Nor can morality be taken from a divine, all-perfect will, because its perfection cannot be known. Whenever an object of the will becomes the basis for prescribing the rule that determines the will, heteronomy results. A contingent law, given by nature, cannot serve as an apodictic moral rule. Instead of autonomy of the will, there would be only heteronomy of the will: the law would be given by means of the subject's nature.

### Section III *(pp. 52–66)* Transition from Metaphysics of Morals to the Critique of Pure Practical Reason

### The Concept of Freedom is the Key to the Explanation of the Autonomy of the Will (pp. 52–3)

Kant explains that the will is a kind of causality of living beings: to the extent that they are rational, and freedom, the autonomy of the will, would enable that causality to operate independently: it is the will's ability of being a law to itself. And this points to one principle only: acting on no other maxim than that which can also have as its object itself as a universal law. However, as this is the formula of the categorical imperative, a free will, and one subject to moral laws, are the same thing.

## Freedom Must Be Presupposed as a Property of the Will of All Rational Beings (pp. 53–4)

But it is not enough to attribute freedom of the will (which cannot be demonstrated) to ourselves, based on human experience, since it must apply to all rational beings. However, it is impossible to think of a rational being accepting direction from outside itself, because its judgements would then be attributable to impulse. So, every rational being must be free, because his will cannot be his own unless it is free.

## Of the Interest Attaching to the Ideas of Morality (pp. 54–8)

Morality has been traced back to the idea of freedom, which must be presupposed, in order to think of a being as rational and possessing a will. But bound up with this idea of freedom is awareness that we must adopt as maxims universal principles, which can serve for our own giving of universal laws. However, why should we, when they have no interest in doing so?

The moral law has been presupposed in the idea of freedom, but its reality has not been proved. This means that there is no satisfactory answer to the question why a maxim's universal validity as a law must be the limiting condition of action. Of course, what would make us worthy to be happy is interesting, but we still do not know why we should freely detach ourselves from all empirical interests, and hold ourselves subject to the moral law.

However, little intelligence is needed to see that all representations that come to us involuntarily, such as those of the senses, enable us to know objects only as they affect us, not as they are in themselves. But we assume that, behind the appearances (the world of sense), there are things in themselves (the world of understanding). As receivers of sensations, we think of ourselves as part of the world of sense, but, when immediately conscious of things, as part of the world of understanding.

Now, human beings have a capacity by which they distinguish themselves from everything else: reason. A rational being must regard himself as intelligence, that is as belonging to the world of understanding. To put it another way, he has two standpoints from which to see the relationship between himself and moral laws. As part of the world of sense, he is subject to laws of nature, but, as part of the world of understanding, he is subject to moral laws that are independent of nature and grounded in reason.

This means that, as a rational being, a human being can only think of the causality of his will under the idea of freedom; and bound up with the idea of freedom are the concept of autonomy and the universal principle of morality. When we think of ourselves as free, we regard ourselves as members of the world of understanding, with an autonomous will and subject to morality. However, when we think of ourselves as placed under obligation, we see ourselves as members of the worlds of both sense and understanding.

### How is a Categorical Imperative Possible? (pp. 58–9)

A rational being can only call his causality a will as a member of the world of understanding. As a member of the world of sense, his actions are determined by desires and inclinations, and so he must regard the laws of the world of understanding as imperatives. Categorical imperatives are possible for him, because the idea of freedom makes him part of the world of understanding; and, if he were only this, his actions would always conform with autonomy of the will. However, since he also belongs to the world of sense, the situation is that they ought to conform with it.

## On the Extreme Boundary of All Practical Philosophy (pp. 59–66)

All human beings consider themselves as having free will, which means that they think of actions that they ought to have done, even though they did not. However, freedom is only an idea of reason, the objective reality of which can be doubted, whereas the existence of nature cannot be doubted. Consequently, there is a dialectic of reason in relation to the will, because the freedom claimed for it seems to contradict the natural necessity of laws of nature. However, the latter is essential in order for us to use reason in our conduct. Thus, we must assume the absence of any real contradiction between freedom and natural necessity in the very same human actions, because we cannot give up either one.

But we shall not be able to understand the possibility of freedom unless this apparent contradiction is eliminated. The claim to freedom of the will is based on our awareness of reason's independence. A human being is subject to determining grounds of an altogether different kind when he thinks of himself as an intelligence, possessing a will, as opposed to a mere phenomenon in the world of sense. He appreciates that there is no contradiction in holding that something, which belongs to the world of sense, and is subject to its laws, is also independent of them as a being in itself. He is subject to laws, given by pure reason, which apply to him immediately and categorically, and, as part of the world of understanding, he does not allow himself to be influenced by the inclinations and desires of the world of sense. Of course, we cannot explain how freedom is possible. The fact is that, where things are no longer determined by laws of nature, there is no possibility of explanation. However, to those who deny the possibility of freedom, and who maintain that the law of nature alone governs human actions, we can only say that things in themselves (though hidden) must lie behind appearances as their ground.

So, a categorical imperative is possible solely through presupposing the idea of freedom. But how freedom itself is possible cannot be seen by human reason; so, we have reached the limits of moral enquiry.

Kant points out that these are important issues of which to be aware, in order to prevent reason looking for the supreme motive of morals in the world of sense, or trying to find it in transcendent concepts, and so losing itself among phantoms. The idea of a world of understanding is valuable, even if knowledge stops as its boundaries. It fosters a keen interest in the moral law, through the ideal of a universal kingdom of ends in themselves (rational beings), of which, by following maxims of freedom as if they were laws of nature, human beings can be members.

### Concluding Remarks (p. 66)

Using reason to speculate on nature results in the absolute necessity of a supreme cause of the world. Our reason also looks for necessity, but can only do so under some condition. It is, therefore, no surprise that reason cannot make the absolute necessity of the categorical imperative comprehensible, because it is not prepared to do so through a condition, such as some interest, as this would mean that it was not the moral law. So, reason is forced just to assume the unconditionally necessary, without being able to make it comprehensible. However, we can at least understand the incomprehensibility of the practical unconditional necessity of the moral imperative, which is all that can be expected when we approach the limits of human reason.

# Glossary

**Absolute necessity.** To be a ground of moral obligation, a moral law or principle must have absolutely binding force.

**Absolute worth.** Complete or unqualified worth. As ends in themselves, human beings have absolute worth.

**Abstraction.** Removal or withdrawal from. To be absolutely good, the will must withdraw from any end to be accomplished, otherwise it will be only relatively good: that is, good in relation to achieving a particular end.

**Agent.** One who performs an action.

**Analytic.** In relation to propositions, it means one where the predicate is included in the subject, or where denying the proposition would be self-contradictory; for example, 'This house is a building'.

**Apodictic.** That which can be proved, and is certain. A maxim, based on interest or inclination, cannot serve as an apodictic moral rule.

*A posteriori.* That which comes after, or is based on, experience/empirical evidence.

**Appearances.** Things as they appear to be, as opposed to things as they are in themselves. See also world of sense, phenomenal world, intellectual world.

*A priori.* That which comes before experience, and which holds (or is claimed to hold) irrespective of experience. According to Kant, moral laws or principles are discovered *a priori* by the reason. So far from being based on experience of the world and human needs, they prescribe standards of conduct for human beings, irrespective of the human condition and general or individual human needs.

**Autonomy (of the will)/principle of autonomy**. The freedom of the will/free will. Kant describes this key idea in his moral philosophy as the supreme principle of morality. Although part of the world of sense or phenomenal world, and subject to laws of nature, human beings, as rational beings, are also part of the intellectual world or noumenal world, and are thus free. Therefore, they are able to subject themselves to moral laws discovered by their reason, and can be held morally responsible for their actions. Kant accepted that the existence of freedom cannot be proved, but, unless it is presupposed, there cannot be moral responsibility. See also causality.

**Beneficence**. Doing good, being actively kind.

**Categorical**. That which is unconditional or absolute.

**Categorical imperative**. The imperative of morality, which commands unconditionally. What it commands must be done for its own sake, and because it is right, not in order to accomplish some further purpose, and it may conflict with a person's inclinations. Kant gives five different formulations of the categorical imperative in the *Groundwork*, the first of which is: 'act only in accordance with that maxim through which you can at the same time will that it become a universal law'.

**Causality**. Acting as a cause, the relation of cause and effect. Kant discusses causality in relation to moral responsibility. As part of the world of sense, human beings are, like everything else, subject to the laws of nature, which suggests that they cannot be held responsible for their actions. However, as rational beings, they belong to the intellectual world, and are subject to moral laws, grounded on reason, which are independent of nature; thus, they are free, and are responsible for their actions.

**Cognize**. Know.

**Common human reason**. The reason, or reasoning capabilities, of ordinary people, as opposed to philosophers. Kant believed that, in general, ordinary people are as likely to be to able distinguish right from wrong as philosophers, although they might not always recognize the influence of their own inclinations on their decisions.

**Concept**. Idea of, understanding of a term, and being able to use it accurately.

**Conditional imperative**. An imperative which commands a course of action, in order to achieve some object, and not for its own sake.

**Conformity**. (In) compliance with. Kant held that, to be morally good, actions must not only comply with the moral law, but be done for its sake.

**Consequence(s)**. See effect and consequentialist system of morals.

**Consequentialist system of morals**. One which, unlike Kant's, decides whether an action is right or wrong on the basis of its consequences. Utilitarianism judges actions to be right to the extent that they promote happiness/pleasure and wrong to the extent that they promote pain. See also deontological system of morals.

**Contingent**. That which depends upon something else, that which might be other than it is.

**Contingent circumstances (of human nature)/contingent conditions (of humanity)**. Kant is referring to human nature as it is, which is the result of a range of empirical factors, which might be otherwise. Therefore, human nature cannot provide the basis for universal moral laws, which apply to all rational beings.

**Contradiction.** In the *Groundwork*, this may refer to a formal contradiction, or to an inconsistency or conflict between two ideas. For example, it would be difficult to adopt the maxim of not helping others when prospering oneself, because, although the human race would survive if this maxim became universal law, it would conflict with itself. There are occasions when one needs the help of others, but such a law would remove any possibility of it.

**Demonstrate.** Proving something conclusively by the use of (arguments derived from) reason.

**Deontological system of morals.** One, such as Kant's, which treats certain actions as being right or wrong in themselves, irrespective of their consequences. Thus, a believer in a deontological moral system would say that it is always wrong to lie, even if, in a particular situation (for example, denying knowledge of the whereabouts of an escaped prisoner of conscience, when asked), lying would produce more happiness (or cause less pain) than telling the truth. See also consequentialist theory of morals.

**Desire(s).** What human beings wish to do. They need to overcome their desire(s), in order to obey the moral law.

**Determinate.** Definite, that which has definite limits.

**Dialectic (of reason).** A debate or discussion. This relates to trying to resolve the apparent contradiction between human beings regarding themselves as having free will when they are also subject to the natural necessity of the world of sense. See also causality.

**Divine will.** God's will. This does not require imperatives in order to obey the moral law, because its will already accords with it.

**Duty.** What all human and rational beings are required to do under the moral law (Kant describes it as the 'objective necessity of an action from obligation'). For Kant, the moral worth of an action, done from duty, lies not in what it accomplishes, but in the maxim upon which it is decided, which must reflect the first formulation of the categorical imperative, and be one which can, at the same time, be willed as a universal law.

**Effect(s).** What results from an action, its consequence(s). For Kant, the rightness or wrongness of an action does not depend on its effects or consequences. An act can be right, even though it accomplishes nothing, and wrong, even though it produces results that are both desirable and good. See also consequentialist system of morals.

**Empirical.** That which relates to, or is based on, experience.

**End.** That which is desired or aimed at.

**End in itself/ends in themselves.** Things or beings that are worthwhile in themselves, and not as means to an end. Human beings and all rational beings are ends in themselves.

**Ethics.** Kant divides ethics, a term which is generally used interchangeably with morality, into an empirical part, which he calls practical anthropology, which concerns the application of morality specifically to human beings, and a rational part, morals, which concerns what all rational beings ought to do.

**Experience.** What relates to the empirical world, and the way that human beings experience things, and which cannot be a source of moral principles.

**Formal.** Concerned with reason and the rules of thinking in general, logic.

**Freedom/freedom of the will/free will/free/freely**. See autonomy of the will.

**God**. See supreme cause of the world.

**Good in itself**. Referring to a good will, which is good in itself and not as means to an end.

**Good will**. A will that carries out moral duties for their own sake, and not for personal advantage, to satisfy desires or inclinations, or because of the consequences. For Kant, a good will is the only thing that is good without qualification.

**Happiness**. Kant considered that people are strongly inclined to happiness, but that it is unattainable, because of the difficulty people have in deciding what would make them happy. They therefore pursue various inclinations, to try to achieve it, but these conflict with each other. Kant makes the interesting points that the more happiness is pursued, the more difficult it is to achieve, and that people who depend on their reason to try to attain it often fare less well than those who rely on instinct. Thus, Kant rejects any idea of trying to relate morality to happiness. However, Kant did believe that, although happiness is not the end of morality, obedience to the moral law for its own sake should be rewarded with happiness, and he develops this point elsewhere in his philosophical writings. See also consequentialist theory of morals and supreme cause of the world.

**Harmonize**. Be in harmony with, fit in with.

**Heteronomy (of the will)**. Kant describes heteronomy of the will as the source of all spurious principles of morality. It arises when the will is determined by inclination(s) or desire(s), not the commands of the moral law, even though what the agent does may comply with morality. Kant gives the example of somebody not lying in order to preserve their reputation, rather than because lying is wrong.

**Holy One of the Gospel**. Jesus. Kant refers to Jesus' teaching that only God is good. However, Kant rejected any idea that what is good is determined by the will of God, or that we know what is good because God has revealed it to us. Rather, it is from rational beings' idea of moral perfection, discovered *a priori* by the reason, and linked inseparably to the concept of a free will, that our concept of God as the highest good comes.

**Holy will**. Like God's will, this does not require imperatives in order to obey the moral law, because its will already accords with the moral law.

**Human beings**. Human beings are rational beings, and as such, and, unlike purely natural beings, are ends in themselves.

**Humanity**. Human beings.

**Human nature**. This belongs to the empirical world, and is subject to inclinations. Therefore, it cannot be the source of moral principles, which must come from the reason.

**Hypothetical imperative**. An imperative, which, unlike a categorical imperative, does not command an action absolutely, but only as a means of achieving another purpose.

**Imperative**. Command, sentence expressing a command.

**Inclination(s)**. What human beings like or desire to do, and which they need to overcome, in order to obey the moral law.

**Inner sensation**. As members of the world of sense, human beings cannot know what they are in themselves through inner sensation, or introspection. This is because they obtain their concept of themselves empirically, not *a priori*, and so the information is part of things as they appear to be, not things as they are in themselves. See also phenomenal world, world of sense, noumenal world, intellectual world.

**Inner worth**. The worth of things that are valuable in themselves. For example, keeping promises and benevolence have inner worth, even if they achieve nothing.

**Instinct**. Natural tendency to behave in a certain way. Kant makes the point that those who follow their instinct are more likely to attain happiness that those who apply reason to the task. In fact, reason has a more important task: to produce a will that is good, not as a means to an end, but in itself.

**Intellectual world**. As rational beings, human beings belong to the intellectual world, the world of understanding, as well as to the world of sense. As part of the world of sense, they are subject to the causality of laws of nature, but, as part of the intellectual world, they are subject to laws that are independent of nature, and which are grounded in reason; thus, they are free to obey the moral law, a law to which they subject themselves. See also autonomy (of the will)/ principle of autonomy.

**Intelligible world**. See intellectual world.

**Interest**. A motive or end for which an action is performed, rather than being done for its own sake. According to Kant, an action cannot be moral if the agent has an interest in performing it, because it has not been done for its own sake.

**Kingdom of ends**. This is the 'moral kingdom', which human beings, as rational beings can create, by always treating themselves and others as ends in themselves, not means. And human beings must always behave as if they are members of such a kingdom.

**Lawgiving**. As rational beings, human beings are givers of the moral law, which has the form of universality. One of the formulations of the categorical imperative is that rational beings should only adopt those maxims that they can also will should become a universal law. They are also subject to the moral law, but it is a law that they give to themselves.

**Law(s)**. In the *Groundwork*, either the moral law(s) or law(s) of nature (depending on context).

**Laws of nature**. Natural laws. As part of the world of sense, human beings are subject to them, but, as members of the intellectual world, they are free in relation to them.

**Logic**. The study of inference and the rules of valid inference.

**Maxim**. A subjective principle or rule of conduct. The maxims human beings adopt must be measured against the categorical imperative, to ensure their fitness to become universal laws, governing the conduct of all rational beings. Maxims must not be based on human needs or inclinations. Those that are must be rejected.

**Means**. That which leads to, gives access to, a certain end.

**Metaphysics**. The investigation of what really exists, of ultimate reality.

**Metaphysics of morals**. Investigation of the general or fundamental principles of morality.

**Mill**, John Stuart (1806–1873). Utilitarian philosopher and author of *Utilitarianism* and *On Liberty*. See also consequentialist system of morals.

**Moral feeling**. A natural tendency to regard certain things as right or wrong, and to do them. According to Kant, it is likely to prove a better (although very imperfect) guide to moral action than pursuing one's own happiness, because it is not subject to any desire for personal advantage.

**Moralist**. One who enquires into, teaches or practises morality

**Morality**. Generally, (principles concerning) what is right and what is wrong. Kant describes it as: 'the relation of actions to the autonomy of the will'.

**Moral law(s)**. The *a priori* moral principles, discovered by reason, which should govern the actions of all rational beings.

**Morally good**. To be morally good, an action must be done for the sake of the moral law, and not merely conform with it.

**Moral obligation**. What one is obliged to do by the moral law. See also obligation.

**Moral philosophy**. Branch of philosophy concerned with moral issues and the general principles of morality. It can be concerned with trying to decide what is right or wrong and why we should adopt/follow a certain set of moral principles, or, more narrowly, with the nature of moral argument (what people are doing when they say that a particular action is right or wrong) and the meaning and use of such moral terms as 'right' and 'good'. Kant believed that its role was to identify *a priori* moral principles.

**Moral principle(s)**. For Kant, an *a priori* principle that enables us to make moral judgements. More generally, the principles or rules of the moral system to which we subscribe.

**Moral responsibility**. Being held accountable for one's actions, and being blamed for acting wrongly. However, this is only possible if human beings are fully free either to follow, or not follow, the moral law.

**Morals**. See ethics.

**Moral worth**. Moral value. Actions have moral value if they are done from duty, not inclination or self-interest. Thus, the charitable acts of one who enjoys helping others lack moral worth, because they are done from inclination, not duty.

**Natural beings**. Beings without reason: animals.

**Nature**. See laws of nature.

**Noumenal world/noumenon(a)**. Things as they are in themselves, as opposed to the phenomenal world, the way that they appear to us. Kant maintained that, as human beings, we experience the world in a particular way, and so do not have knowledge of things as they are in themselves. See also world of sense, intellectual world.

**Objective reality**. Whether something actually exists, whether something exists in reality. For Kant, freedom is essential to morality and moral responsibility, but whether it actually exists cannot be proved.

**Object of the will**. Something the will is aiming at, an interest, which means that the will is determined by something other than the moral law, resulting in heteronomy of the will.

**Obligation**. What human and all rational beings are required to do by the moral law, which is found, not in human nature, or the empirical world, but in the concepts of pure reason.

**Ontological**. To do with being, what exists, the essence of things.

**Ought**. Indicates duty or obligation, what somebody should do.

**Person**. Rational being, end in itself, who is of absolute worth.

**Phenomenal world/phenomenon(a)**. Kant distinguished between the phenomenal world, the world as it appears to us, due to the way that we, as human beings, experience it, and the noumenal world, things as they are in themselves, of which we cannot have experience, because of the kind of beings we are. See also world of sense, intellectual world.

**Philanthropist**. One who helps other people.

**Philosopher**. One who studies and practises/teaches philosophy. Kant makes the point that ordinary people are as likely to be right in their moral judgements as philosophers, but the later have a role in showing how morality works.

**Philosophy**. Literally, love of wisdom. The study of ultimate reality, what really exists, the most general principles of things.

**Philosophy of religion**. Application of philosophical methods to religious concepts, beliefs and arguments.

**Physics**. Study of the laws of nature.

**Practical anthropology**. The empirical part of ethics, concerned with the application of morality specifically to human beings.

**Practical law(s)**. An action-prescribing law, which, as it is based on the categorical imperative, is a moral law.

**Practical reason**. Reason when it is investigating or considering matters of morality.

**Practical rule**. An action-guiding rule, but which, as it is not based on the categorical imperative, is not a moral law.

**Precept**. Command or maxim.

**Principle of action**. See maxim.

**Principle of autonomy**. See autonomy (of the will).

**Principle of the will**. This refers to moral principles.

**Prudent/prudence**. Cautious or sensible, relating to conduct which, although it conforms with duty, may lack moral worth. Kant gives the example of a shopkeeper, who does not overcharge his customers. He may be doing so, not because honesty is right, but because, by not overcharging them, he keeps his customers. Kant also refers to the hypothetical imperative or precept of prudence, relating to skill in choosing our own greatest well-being.

**Rational**. See reason/pure reason.

**Rational being**. Any being possessing reason. Kant makes the point that the moral law would apply to any rational being, not just to human beings.

**Reason/pure reason**. The rational capacity, the ability to reason, possessed by human beings, and which distinguishes them from animals. Reason enables human beings (and any other rational beings) to be free, because they can conduct their lives according to *a priori* moral principles of the reason, instead of being governed by desires and inclinations.

**Representation (of the law)**. This refers to the fact that only rational beings freely subject themselves to the moral law of reason, and have the moral law as the determining ground of their will.

**Self-determination**. This refers to the determining ground of the will, which may be a relative end, a specific effect or something that is an end in itself, and which therefore has absolute worth.

**Self-interest**. What is done for personal advantage, rather than out of duty, even though it may conform with duty. See also prudent/prudence.

**Senses**. See world of sense.

**Speculative philosophy**. Philosophical enquiry. Kant is specifically concerned with the issue of how to reconcile human beings' freedom to obey the moral law with their being subject to laws of nature.

**Spurious principles of morality**. False principles of morality. See also heteronomy (of the will).

**Sublime/sublimity**. What is impressive or awe-inspiring about something. Kant writes that it is when the maxims adopted are independent of any advantage that might be achieved from following them that they have sublimity.

**Supreme cause of the world**. God. In the *Groundwork*, Kant states that the use of reason to speculate about nature results in an absolute necessity: that of a supreme cause of the world. Although the moral law is completely independent of God's will, and must be obeyed for its own sake, and not to please God, Kant, in his *Critique of Practical Reason* and *Religion with the Boundaries of Mere Reason*, argues that God is nonetheless a necessary assumption, in order to make sense of morality. We need to postulate God, if, ultimately, obedience to the moral law is to be rewarded with happiness. God (along with freedom and immortality) is what Kant calls a postulate of the practical reason.

**Supreme norm.** The supreme standard of morality, the *a priori* moral law.

**Supreme principle of morality.** See autonomy (of the will).

**Synthetic proposition.** This is a proposition, which gives actual information. Generally, it is believed that synthetic propositions are also *a posteriori*, that is derive the information they give from experience. However, Kant maintained that there are also *a priori* synthetic propositions, such as those of morality. These convey information, but it comes from the reason, not experience. See also *a priori, a posteriori.*

**Temptation to transgression of duty.** That which leads us not to do our duty.

**Theological.** That which relates to God.

**Things in themselves.** See noumenal world.

**Transcendent concepts.** That which is above or apart from the material or empirical world, that which relates to God. Kant warns that moral principles are not to be found in the world of sense, the empirical world, or in transcendent concepts, but in the reason.

**Unconditional.** Has no condition attached to it, does not depend for its fulfilment on something else. The categorical imperative commands unconditionally.

**Universal law.** A moral law that applies universally to all rational beings. A rational being ought never to act except in such a way that he could also will that his maxim become a universal law.

## Glossary

**Universal law of nature**. One of the formulations of the categorical imperative is: 'act as if the maxim of your action were to become by your will a universal law of nature'.

**Utilitarianism**. See consequentialist system of morals.

**Volition**. Act of willing.

**Will**. The capability of wishing for something and using one's mental powers to try to accomplish it.

**World of sense**. The empirical world, the world as it appears to us. See also phenomenal world, appearances.

**World of understanding**. See intellectual world.